HOW TO DRAW

PETS

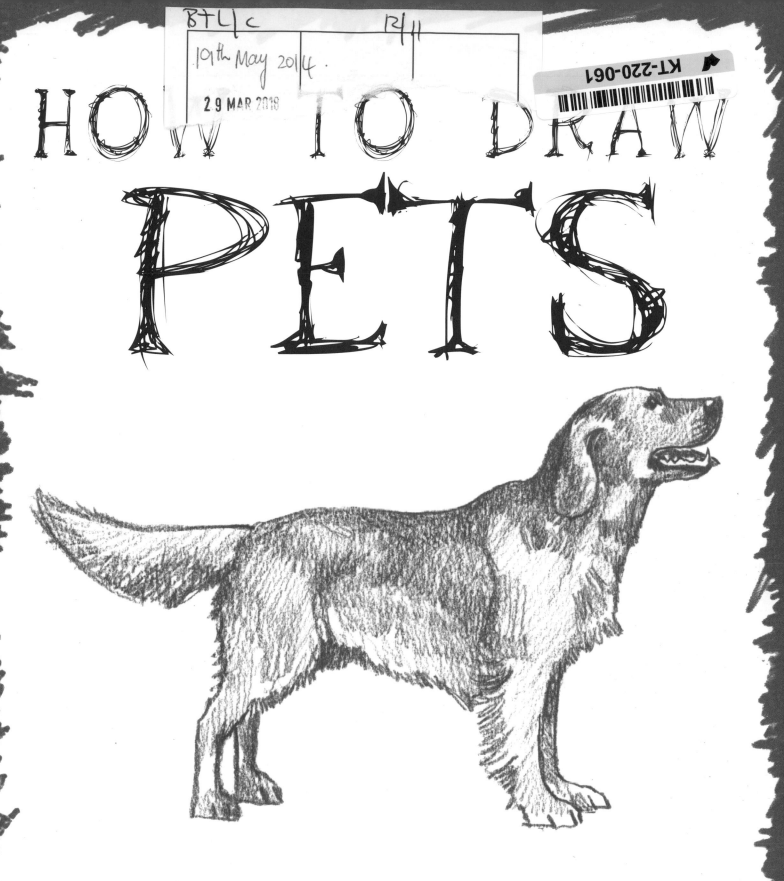

Mark Bergin

BOOK HOUSE

SALARIYA

Published in Great Britain in MMXII by
Book House, an imprint of
The Salariya Book Company Ltd
25 Marlborough Place, Brighton BN1 1UB

1 3 5 7 9 8 6 4 2

Please visit our website at **www.salariya.com**
for **free** electronic versions of:
You Wouldn't Want to Be an Egyptian Mummy!
You Wouldn't Want to Be a Roman Gladiator!
You Wouldn't Want to Be a Polar Explorer!
**You Wouldn't Want to Sail on a 19th-Century
   Whaling Ship!**

Author: Mark Bergin was born in Hastings in 1961.
He studied at Eastbourne College of Art and has
specialised in historical reconstructions as well as
aviation and maritime subjects since 1983. He lives
in Bexhill-on-Sea with his wife and three children.

Editor: Rob Walker

PB ISBN: 978-1-907184-65-9

A CIP catalogue record for this
book is available from the
British Library.

Printed and bound in China.
Printed on paper from
sustainable sources.

**WARNING: Fixatives should be
used only under adult supervision.**

Visit our websites to read interactive free web
books, stay up to date with new releases, catch
up with us on the Book House Blog, view our
electronic catalogue and more!

www.book-house.co.uk
Information books and graphic novels

www.scribobooks.com
Fiction books

www.scribblersbooks.com
Books for babies, toddlers and pre-school
children.

Follow us on Facebook and
Twitter by visiting
www.salariya.com

PAPER FROM
SUSTAINABLE
FORESTS

Contents

Making a start

Learning to draw is about looking and seeing. Keep practising and get to know your subject. Use a sketchbook to make quick drawings. Start by doodling and experimenting with shapes and patterns. There are many ways to draw; this book shows only some methods. Visit art galleries, look at artists' drawings, see how friends draw, but above all, find your own way.

Make a range of
sketches, from detailed
drawings to quick
sketches trying to
capture the form of
the animal as quickly
and accurately as
possible.

Yellow

Green

Blue

Yellow

Red

Grey

Yellow

Make a note of any of your
subjects' features which may help
later when doing a finished drawing,
such as its colouring and any
outstanding features.

Drawing materials

Try using different types of drawing paper and materials. Experiment with charcoal, wax crayons and pastels. All pens, from felt-tips to ballpoints, will make interesting marks — you could also try drawing with pen and ink on wet paper.

Felt-tip

Silhouette is a style of drawing that uses only a solid black shape.

Ink

Lines drawn in **ink** cannot be erased, so keep your ink drawings sketchy and less rigid. Don't worry about mistakes as these lines can be lost in the drawing as it develops.

Hard **pencils** are greyer and soft pencils are blacker. Hard pencils are graded from 6H (the hardest) through 5H, 4H, 3H and 2H to H. Soft pencils are graded from B, 2B, 3B, 4B and 5B up to 6B (the softest).

Charcoal is very soft and can be used for big, bold drawings. Ask an adult to spray your charcoal drawings with fixative to prevent smudging.

Pastels are even softer than charcoal, and come in a wide range of colours. Ask an adult to spray your pastel drawing with fixative to prevent it from smudging.

Perspective

If you look at any object from different viewpoints, you will see that the part that is closest to you looks larger, and the part furthest away from you looks smaller. Drawing in perspective is a way of creating a feeling of depth – of showing three dimensions on a flat surface.

The vanishing point (V.P.) is the place in a perspective drawing where parallel lines appear to meet. The position of the vanishing point depends on the viewer's eye level. Sometimes a low viewpoint can give your drawing added drama.

V.P.

V.P.

V.P.   V.P.

Two-point perspective uses two
vanishing points: one for lines running along
the length of the subject, and one on
the opposite side for lines running across
the width of the subject.

Three-point perspective uses a
third vanishing point for lines
running vertically up or down.
This gives a very realistic three-
dimensional effect.

V.P.   V.P.

High eye level
(view from above)

V.P.

V.P. = vanishing point

9

Heads, paws and claws

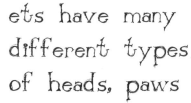

Pets have many
different types
of heads, paws
and claws. Studying and sketching
the detailed features of a pet will
help you with your final drawings.

Quick pencil sketches can help
you to understand the structure
of paws and claws.

Look for areas where tone
should be darker and also
for changes of texture.

The more you study a
subject and practise drawing
it, the more accurate your
drawings will become.

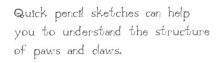

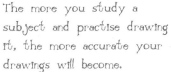

Try to capture as much detail
as you can in your sketches.

Look carefully at the size and
shape of the eyes, ears and nose.
Note the length of the whiskers.

Always consider the light source and
add tone to the darker areas.

Using photos

Drawing from photographs of pets can help you develop both your drawing skills and your eye for detail.

Make a tracing of a photograph and draw a grid of squares on it.

Now take a piece of drawing paper of the same proportions and draw another grid on it, either enlarging or reducing the squares' size, You can now copy the shapes from each square of the tracing to the drawing paper, using the grid to guide you.

Light source

Light source

To make your drawing look three-dimensional, decide which side the light source is coming from, and put in areas of shadow where the light doesn't reach.

Sketch in an overall tone and add surrounding textures to create interest and a sense of movement. Pay attention to the position of your drawing on the paper; this is called composition.

13

Dog

Dogs are often kept as domestic pets but some, like sheepdogs, are used for work.

Head

Front legs

Hind legs

Draw a circle for the head. Draw two ovals, the larger one for the top of the front legs and the other for the top of the hind legs.

Join the two ovals and the circle with simple lines.

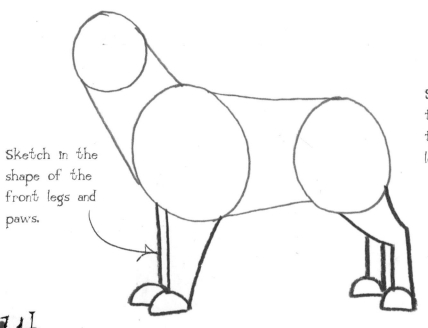

Sketch in the shape of the front legs and paws.

Sketch in the basic shape of the hind legs, remembering that the top half of each leg curves outwards.

14

Add a curved shape
for the ear.

Draw the shape of
the tail with
curved lines.

Sketch in
construction
lines to place
the snout.

Sketch in darker areas of fur
to help define the shape of the
dog's muscles.

Draw in the dog's
snout, adding its
teeth and nose.

Start to add fur
to the body.

Complete the details
of the head.

Add lines to the feet
to define the paws.

Add areas of short lines to
create the fur texture on the
dog's body.

Remove any unwanted
construction lines with
an eraser.

15

Cat

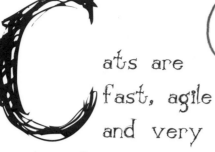

Cats are fast, agile and very independent animals. They are one of the most popular pets.

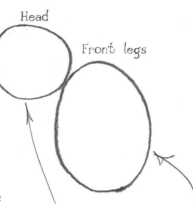

Head

Front legs

Hind legs

Draw a circle for the head. Draw two ovals for the top of the front legs and the top of the hind legs. The circle for the head should be touching the front oval.

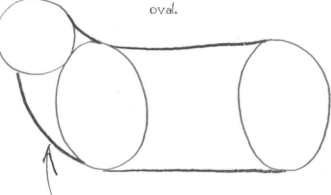

Join the ovals and the circle with simple lines.

Draw the shape of the front legs with semi—circles for the paws.

Sketch the shape of the rear legs with the top halves curving outwards. Add semi—circles for the paws.

Position triangular shapes on top of the head for ears, circles for eyes and basic shapes for the mouth and nose.

Add two long lines for the tail.

Add lines to define the paws.

Complete the head details: add short hair inside each ear and whiskers on each side of the face.

Shade in the cat's eyes and leave a lighter area around them to help them stand out.

A series of short lines gives the cat striped fur.

Add jagged lines around some edges of the cat's body to create fur.

Remove any unwanted construction lines with an eraser.

17

Hamster

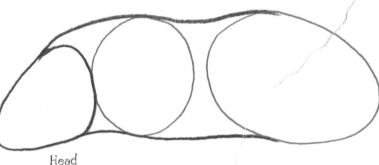

Small, furry hamsters have large cheek pouches for carrying food.

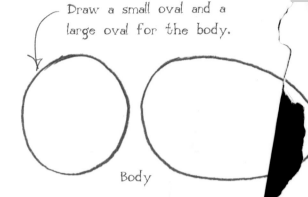

Draw a small oval and a large oval for the body.

Body

Draw in the head shape touching the first oval. Join all three shapes together with curved lines.

Head

Sketch in the position of the hamster's ears, eyes, nostrils and mouth.

Add a short stubby tail.

Draw in the basic shape of the paws.

Shade in the eyes and the inside of the ears.

Add areas of tone to the body shape to suggest fur.

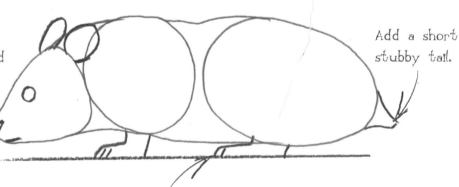

Remove any unwanted construction lines.

18

Complete the details of the paws.

Add darker shading to areas that light would not reach.

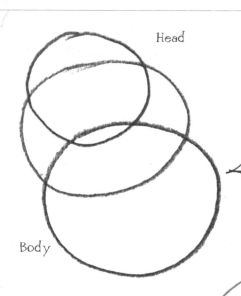

Head

Body

Draw overlapping circles and ovals for the head and body.

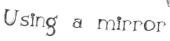

Using a mirror

You can often see mistakes more easily by looking at the drawing in reverse, using a mirror.

Add two small ovals for paws and connect them to the body with curved lines.

Draw in the basic paw shapes.

Sketch in the position of the ears, eyes, nose and mouth.

Complete the head details by adding dark tone to the ears and the eyes.

Complete the body shape by adding curved lines.

Draw in jagged lines around the hamster for a furry texture.

Add lines to define the paws.

Leave some of the hamster's belly mostly white to suggest fur colour.

Use an eraser to remove any unwanted construction lines.

19

Rabbit

Rabbits are popular pets that are usually kept outside in a hutch.

Draw a circle for the head and two ovals for the shoulders and rear.

Head

Shoulders

Rear

Draw two long connecting curved lines.

Add two front legs using straight lines, and use half circles for the front paws.

Sketch in the basic shape of the rear legs and paws.

Composition

By framing your drawing with a square or a rectangle you can make it look completely different.

Position the rabbit's ears on its head.

Sketch in the rabbit's muzzle using straight lines.

Add a little round tail.

This drawing of a rabbit from a different angle shows all the construction lines used.

Add the head details: draw in the ears, eyes, small nose and mouth.

Add tone to the rabbit's body to give the impression of fur.

Add shading to areas where the light would not reach.

Remove any unwanted construction lines using an eraser.

Fish

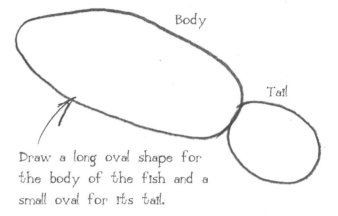

Pet fish are often highly decorative and brightly coloured.

Draw a long oval shape for the body of the fish and a small oval for its tail.

Body

Tail

Add a series of curved lines for the fins.

Add a small circle for the eye and put a dot in the middle.

Draw in curved lines to show the pattern on the fish's body.

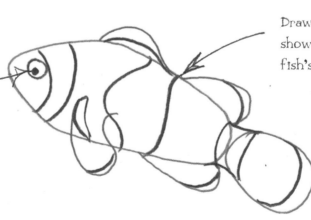

Add tone to define the pattern and to create darker areas of shading.

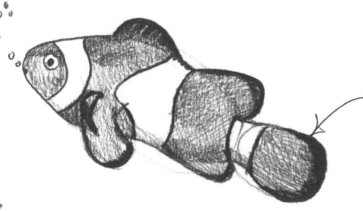

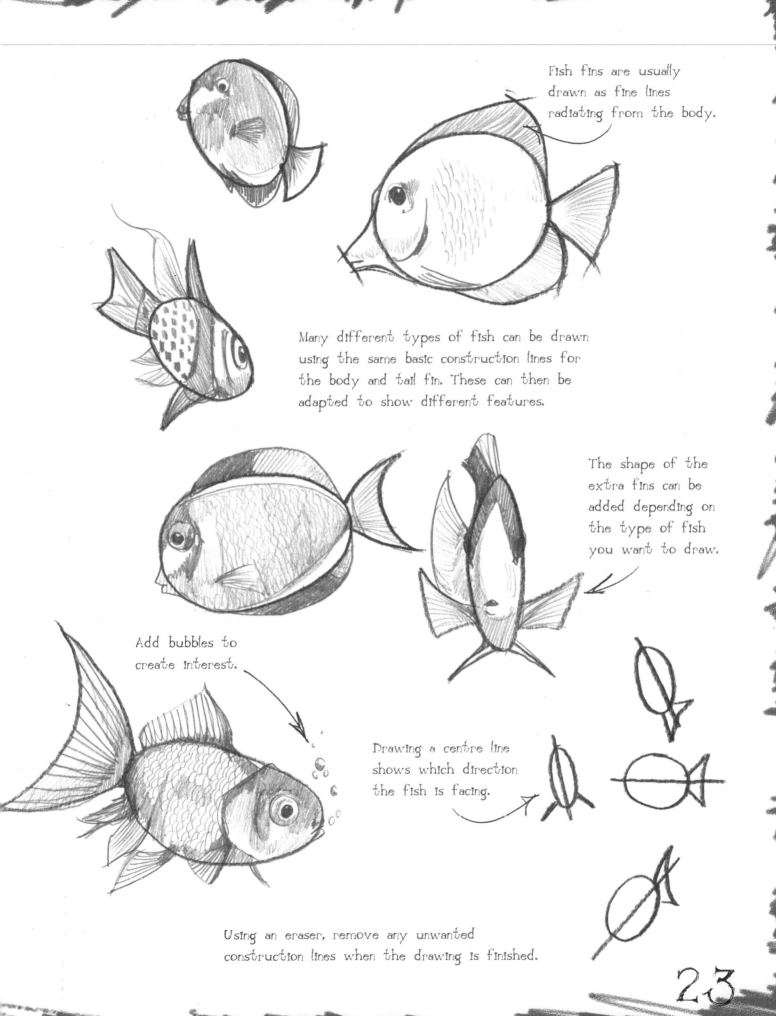

Fish fins are usually drawn as fine lines radiating from the body.

Many different types of fish can be drawn using the same basic construction lines for the body and tail fin. These can then be adapted to show different features.

The shape of the extra fins can be added depending on the type of fish you want to draw.

Add bubbles to create interest.

Drawing a centre line shows which direction the fish is facing.

Using an eraser, remove any unwanted construction lines when the drawing is finished.

23

Parrot

Parrots are large, colourful birds that can often mimic a person's speech.

Head

Draw two ovals for the parrot's head and body.

Body

Join the head to the body with two curved lines.

Sketch in a simple tube shape as a perch.

Draw in the shape of the tail with two long lines.

Draw the basic shape of the claws around the perch.

Sketch in long curved lines to add the wing shape.

24

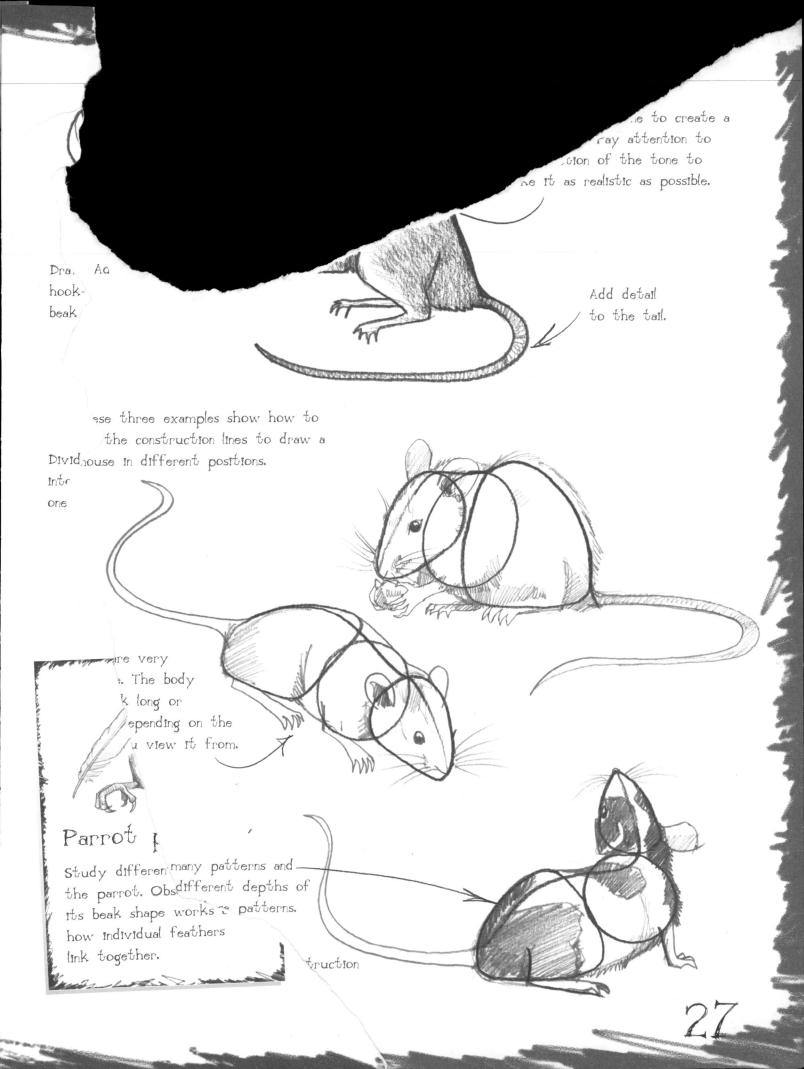

...e to create a
...ray attention to
...tion of the tone to
...ke it as realistic as possible.

Dra. Aa
hook-
beak

Add detail
to the tail.

...se three examples show how to
... the construction lines to draw a
Divid ...ouse in different positions.
int...
one

...re very
... The body
...k long or
...epending on the
...u view it from.

Parrot

Study differen...many patterns and
the parrot. Obs...different depths of
its beak shape works... patterns.
how individual feathers
link together.

...truction

27

many p... to others th... make great pets.

long curvy line for the snake's spine.

Add an oval for the head.

On either side of the spine draw another two long lines for the body which taper together at the tail end.

Add in the shape of the snake's head (see instructions below).

Complete the head details, adding its eyes, nostrils and tongue.

Add tone to the snake's body to give it a distinctive pattern.

Add shadow under the snake depending on the direction of the light source.

A snake's head has a distinctive shape. Create a construction line box as shown here to help you draw the head and features.

A drawing of a snake's head from the side shows the raised areas and position of the features.

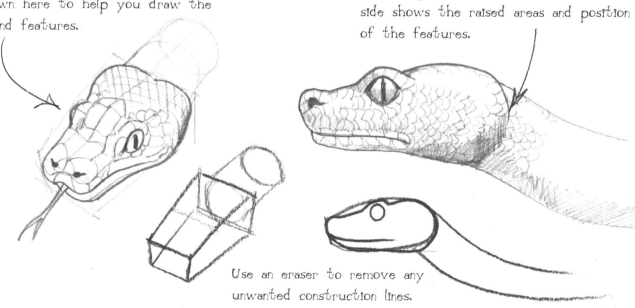

Use an eraser to remove any unwanted construction lines.

29

Bearded dragon

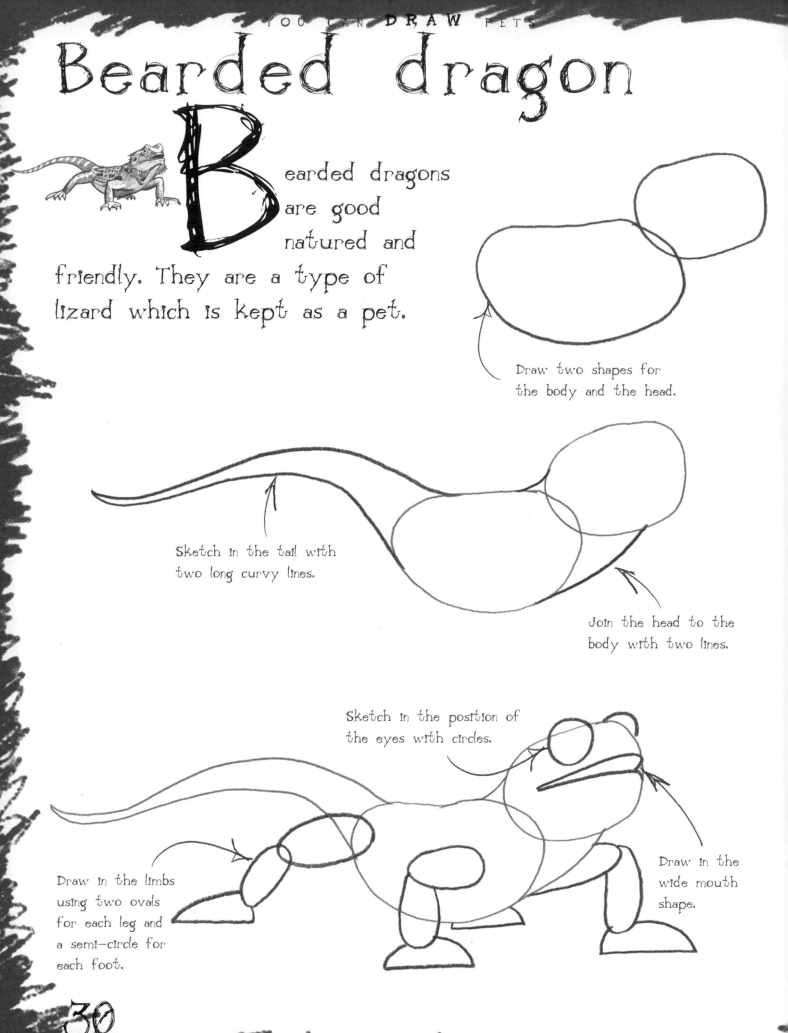

Bearded dragons are good natured and friendly. They are a type of lizard which is kept as a pet.

Draw two shapes for the body and the head.

Sketch in the tail with two long curvy lines.

Join the head to the body with two lines.

Sketch in the position of the eyes with circles.

Draw in the wide mouth shape.

Draw in the limbs using two ovals for each leg and a semi-circle for each foot.

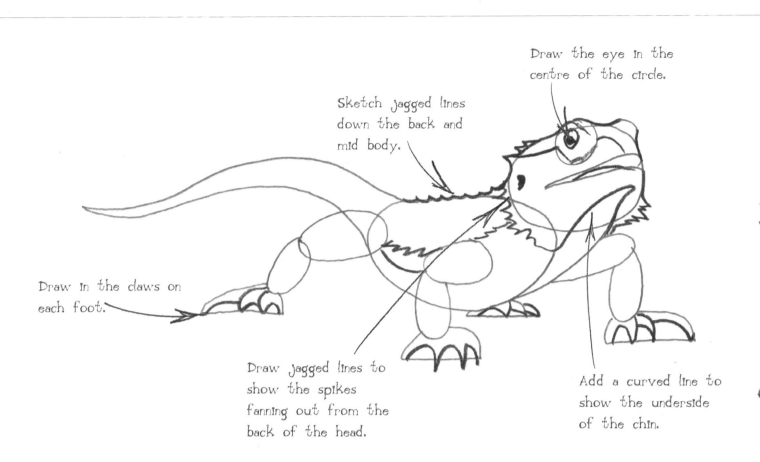

Draw the eye in the centre of the circle.

Sketch jagged lines down the back and mid body.

Draw in the claws on each foot.

Draw jagged lines to show the spikes fanning out from the back of the head.

Add a curved line to show the underside of the chin.

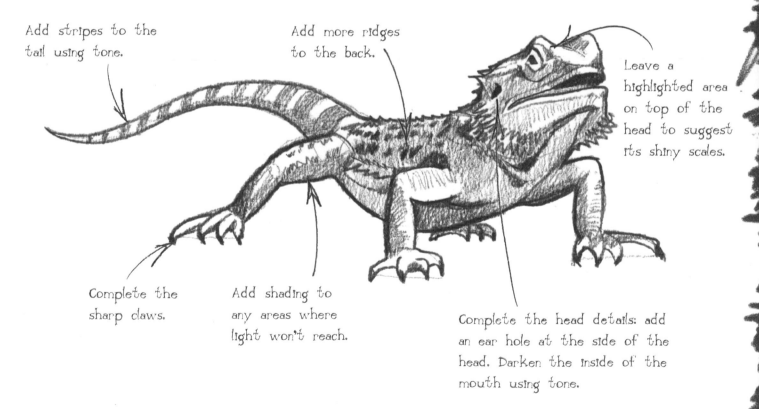

Add stripes to the tail using tone.

Add more ridges to the back.

Leave a highlighted area on top of the head to suggest its shiny scales.

Complete the sharp claws.

Add shading to any areas where light won't reach.

Complete the head details: add an ear hole at the side of the head. Darken the inside of the mouth using tone.

Remove any unwanted construction lines with an eraser.

Glossary

Composition The arrangement of the parts of a picture on the drawing paper.

Construction lines Guidelines used in the early stages of a drawing. They are usually erased later.

Fixative A type of resin used to spray over a finished drawing to prevent smudging. **It should only be used by an adult.**

Light source The direction from which the light seems to come in a drawing.

Perspective A method of drawing in which near objects are shown larger than faraway objects to give an impression of depth.

Pose The position assumed by a figure.

Proportion The correct relationship of scale between each part of the drawing.

Silhouette A drawing that shows only a flat dark shape, like a shadow.

Vanishing point The place in a perspective drawing where parallel lines appear to meet.

Index